# ANIMALS IN
# THE SPIRIT WORLD

by

## HAROLD SHARP

First Published in 1966 by the
Spiritualist Association of Great Britain

First published 1966 by
Spiritualist Association of Great Britain

This edition 2018
Saturday Night Press Publications
England

snppbooks@gmail.com
www.snppbooks.com

ISBN 978 1 908421 28 9

*Cover design*: *Ann Harrison, SNPP.*
*Photographs*: Elephant, Cat, Dog - © Ann Harrison;  Harold Sharp -
from original cover; Sparrow-copyright free; Monkey-not attrib.

## A Note from the Publisher

The medium Harold Sharp was best known for his spiritually inspired drawings known as auragraphs.

I first heard of him in 1993 through Tom Harrison, who had in his possession auragraphs drawn for himself and his wife, Doris in 1953. At the time I too was drawing auragraphs, in a very different form, and I was fascinated by the beautiful colours and style that Harold Sharp used, but I knew nothing of his life or interests.

In 2009, when I was asked to republish *Faces of the Living Dead* by Paul Miller – about the spirit portrait artist Frank Leah – I discovered a reference to Harold Sharp and a drawing of his life-long spirit companion Brother Peter.

Then in 2018, through a chance comment on social media, (is anything in this life by chance?) I discovered that Harold Sharp had written a beautiful account of animals in the spirit world. Unfortunately, the book was out of print and the few available copies were woefully expensive.

Thankfully, with the help of Karl Jackson Barnes, who had an original 1966 edition, we have been able to bring Harold Sharp's wonderful little book back to life, for everyone who has 'lost' a dear animal friend or companion. Where possible we have kept to his style of punctuation.

I wish you a happy reunion when your time comes to join them.

Ann Harrison
Saturday Night Press Publications

March 2018

# Foreword to the First Edition

As a great lover of animals and one who has "lost" many dogs and cats, I am delighted that Harold Sharp has written this book. It will bring happiness to many who have "loved and lost" their four-legged friends. After reading these pages we need no longer wonder whether we shall ever be with our faithful friends again for we shall know that they have survived death just as we shall when our call comes.

I have worked with Harold Sharp for nearly 30 years and have grown to respect and esteem him greatly. He loves all life, and cruelty and brutality are loathsome to him. His wonderful gifts as a medium have brought comfort and encouragement to countless people and his knowledge of the Spirit World has been the means of greatly assisting those who mourn.

He has written this book in his inimitable and homely way and those of us who know him well can imagine him talking to us as we read. I feel that all who love animals and birds are indebted to him for placing on record the incidents described in this book.

T. Ralph Rossiter,

Secretary,

The Spiritualist Association of Great Britain.

20th January, 1966

Brother Peter
(as drawn by Frank Leah)

## ANIMALS IN THE SPIRIT WORLD

I was visiting an aged crippled woman who for some years had been bedridden and we had been discussing the afterlife and the perfect naturalness of it.

"Well, you know," she said, "I never could swallow the usual idea of Heaven—Golden floors and pearly gates and harps all round, it always seemed very far-fetched to me. If I can have my old Jumbo there, I shall be perfectly happy."

Jumbo was a faithful old Shepherd dog who, during the six years of her paralysis had been her constant and loving companion. She loved Jumbo and I am sure the dog loved her quite as dearly. When the dog at a great age died it was but the prelude to her passing too.

Sometime afterwards I had a sitting with Mrs Neville — in those days a well-known London Medium and she said —among other things—"There is a woman here and she is about 60 years of age. She is saying 'Chester'—that is probably her name or the name of the town where she lived. She has a big shaggy dog with her, she calls him Jumbo. She is dressed in tweeds and is just off for a walk with her dog. My word, they are an energetic pair."

How wonderful. How pleasing. It was most surely my old friend with her old companion. How right is the old scripture which tells of the other world as a painless zone where distress and sorrow are unknown. Sarah Chester's paralysis —a thing of the past—a not too pleasant memory of her earth plane days. And the stiffened old age of Jumbo is also a thing forgotten.

When I was telling this story to an agnostic recently he appeared to be highly amused—"Good gracious, what nonsense," he said "You surely do not believe that dead people live on and that animals do too?" I said, "Yes, I know they do." His answer to that—rather crudely put, was, " My God, where do they put them all? "

It is very surprising how man, in his immature imagination limits the limitlessness of the spiritual realms. If he would only pause to consider for a moment, he would begin to realise something of the majestic extent of our own material Universe—which in comparison to the illimitable Spirit World, is puny indeed.

Think of this for a moment, if I may digress—I read on Christmas Eve (1964) that the new automatic station called Zond II which the Soviet Union has projected to prove outer space has already, at terrific speed, travelled more than three million miles from earth and is still rushing forward through the void, its signals still carrying detailed information faultlessly back to earth. This is truly wonderful. It has been achieved by the skill of man. But if man-made instruments can work so wonderfully, is it not likely that the instruments that the God of Nature has devised can work even more wonderfully? Man's delicate psychic projector and recorder is a wonderful provision. It can sweep the eternal planes of Spirit and bring back to the dwellers on earth both comfort and enlightenment.

"There are more things in Heaven and Earth, Horatio, than are dreamed of in your philosophy," said Shakespeare. How very true.

Every living thing has an aura of magnetic power or energy, radiating from it. This is not visible to the physical eye—the aura reveals a great deal. For instance the aura of an animal lover is suffused with an orange radiance. These rays are extremely soothing to animals. They inspire trust and confidence. They attract animals, much as a magnet will attract steel. Fear, on the other hand, fills the aura with turgid brown which to animals is an irritant which stimulates anger and a desire to attack.

Since there is no death to any form of Life, your animal friends live on as surely as do your human friends. It is only the physical sheath which has been discarded and buried and if your orange ray has ever stirred joy, and a feeling of affinity in any creature while it was "in the body pent", rest assured that your ray will still attract and your pet which is living a far more active and completely fearless life than when on earth— is still drawn to your side, even as it was before it 'died'.

A Medium—a psychic—one equipped with a rapid receiving set can actually see this taking place. Just as his physical eyes can see the material things around him, his psychic sight can tune in to that finer wavelength—the spiritual realm, which poets call Heaven.

I first became aware of this psychic faculty operating when I was seven years of age. An old monk would frequently appear sitting in the armchair by my bed, seemingly deep in thought or meditation. I always felt happy and comforted in his presence. As far as I can remember he never spoke to me during these nocturnal visits. Occasionally, a choirboy came and sang—but not so frequently as the monk—and as for Myrtle, my own little Pekinese, who my father was compelled to shoot as it had a

11

malignant and painful growth, she for some long time after her 'death' would jump on to my bed and nestle close to me just as she had always done.

Because this psychic gift is a natural gift all this seemed quite normal to me, though my parents—not being psychic— became very worried if I mentioned these things as I think they thought it very abnormal. It wasn't until I was seventeen that, coming to live in London, I came in contact with Spiritualists and became a serious investigator of the most important and far reaching subject in the world—The Indestructability of Life.

My experiences with the monk and others were only explainable because a part of me, my psychic part, was registering an impact made by living beings from another sphere another 'wave-length'—whose indestructible lives still function in a perfectly natural way, in spiritual bodies, in spite of the fact that their earth plane bodies had been buried long before.


I have been asked to tell you about some of the animals—and birds—I have met who live beyond death, in that vast, rarely seen—excepting by the clairvoyant—Spiritual Universe of God. We want you who love animals, or who have lost some pet dear to you, to realise that they still live, happy and carefree in a most wonderful realm. I want you to realise too, that everytime you think of them or speak of them, it is as though, through your orange ray, you called "Come." And they do come. Do not let them find you sad. That would make them feel sad, too.

Some years ago a dear good soul came to me for a sitting, very distressed; her mother had had a cat which she loved dearly and before her death she had asked her only daughter to care for it. The daughter willingly promised but in time the cat became seriously ill and in such pain that the vet declared that the only kindly course was to have it put to sleep. Reluctantly she consented, but since its death she had been very troubled in conscience for breaking—as she thought—her promise to her mother. My Guide, Brother Peter, commenced the sitting thus—"Your mother is here. She understands perfectly and is very grateful to you for sending "Tips" to her, where it can never feel pain, and as she received it on her birthday, it was just like receiving a birthday present. It has no pain now, she wants to stress that it is happy and full of life. She is so delighted to have it with her." The effect upon the sitter was wonderful; a gnawing anxiety which day by day she had magnified out of all proportion had completely disappeared, making her world seem brighter.

Before that wonderful materialising medium, Jack Webber, came to live in London, he stayed with me several times in my Hampstead flat and gave a series of materialising séances there. He did not know how fond of monkeys I am and that when living in my old home in Leicestershire I had kept several as pets. My favourite was a blue mangaby who, though very lovable was exceedingly sensitive and vain—ever seeking to attract attention and admiration. His name was Mickey. It ought to have been Mickey Mischief for he was constantly disturbing the peace with his delightfully naughty pranks. One Sunday morning he escaped, galloped down the village street and attracted, no doubt, by the singing of the choir, ran into the church, leapt on to the pulpit where he had espied a candle and to the Rector's indignation refused to move until he had eaten the whole of it. He always regarded candles as a great delicacy.

A monkey's perspiration contains a certain proportion of saltpetre which crystalises on the skin. They are very fond of eating this and when bored they often pass the time away by searching through their fur, seeking these tasty savoury morsels. People who do not understand, imagine that they are searching for fleas. If anyone accused Mickey of flea-hunting he felt it a great indignity and became really angry.

Now back to Webber and one of the Hampstead séances. Reubin, a control with a lovely voice had just finished singing when I became aware of a considerable weight on my knee. Black-Cloud, Webber's Guide, said—"Do not move, Mr Sharp, there is a lovely large monkey materialising on your knee." It gradually became visible— Mickey—but unfortunately, Black-Cloud suddenly cried loudly, "No, No, Mickey, you must not catch fleas in public." That was enough for Mickey— with one bound he had gone to where— I hope— no one would misunderstand.

On another occasion, Webber had been to a football match and was later than usual coming home. The Circle gathered and waited, passing the time away in pleasant chatter. The talk turned to the plight of wild birds in the wintry weather and one sitter thought that I did very wrongly to buy a large loaf daily for birds while so many human beings were starving. When later Webber arrived and the séance commenced a lovely cock blackbird, with his orange beak glowing, materialised and whistled a truly magnificent song.

When it had finished Black-Cloud said, "He was singing you a thank you on behalf of the birds you feed."

Very much more recently another blackbird came back from "The Sunny Sphere". For a year or more a hen blackbird with only one leg regularly visited my "feeding ground".

As the other blackbirds often attacked her, I took to feeding her alone—away from the others in my porch, standing guard to keep the others at bay if they wished to interfere. This bird became so tame that it would eat cheese—its favourite dainty—out of my hand, and even from time to time it would come uninvited to pick up crumbs on my kitchen floor. As it could only hop along, I called it "Hoppy". At any time of the day I had only to go into the garden and call, "Hoppy, Hoppy," and from wherever it might be, it would come to me. It knew 7 o'clock in the morning as surely as a drunkard knows 'opening time' — for at 7, the loaf, crumbled into small pieces, is scattered. If, for any reason, I was a few minutes late, Hoppy would be in the porch pecking at the door and crying loudly "Quelp! Quelp! Quelp!"

Then early in the New Year there came a day when Hoppy did not come. I called and still no response. Over and over again I went into the garden and called. At last one conclusion only was possible. Some cat must have killed it.

A fortnight or so later as I was leaving my breakfast, my psychic equipment registered a familiar note, "Quelp! Quelp!" and clairvoyantly, in a wonderfully clear vision I saw her on the chair rail that she delighted to perch upon— and as she hopped towards me, I noticed that now she had two legs. I think that perhaps that was what she wanted me to see. It is only upon the earth plane that cripplings can take place—the vibrations are slow—adjustments are slow— habit deformity too often takes complete control. But in the spiritual realm Divine Law operates without material hinderance.

15

We were a farming family at home, but because as a youth I could not endure the practice of breeding animals that we might enrich ourselves by slaughtering them, I left home and became a journalist in London. Little did I realise what an important step this was to be, but there came a day when thanks to a group of wise and kindly folk, I was shown that even in London among all the houses and streets and smoke and smells and rush and tear and excitement, there was a gigantic invisible door to a wonderful invisible realm—a door to which everyone had been given an invisible key—hidden from view, it is true, but they who, with patience, would seek it would surely find it. When they had opened the door, the vast once unseen world lay open to their view, a world of splendour unimaginable—a world where "There is no Death" is demonstrated—A World of Life Unending. A World adjacent to everyone but so little suspected. How grateful I am to those dear kind friends who encouraged me to seek the key. What joy, what understanding it has brought. At first I opened the door in sheer curiosity. Then came a phase of wonder at the majesty of it all, and at last I was encouraged to enter and to mingle with the ever-living ones—for short visits it is true, but these enabled me to understand more and more that the 'inner side of life'— the 'invisible realms' with its wonderful laws, is far more wonderful than the material husk which for so long has obscured our view.

When my sister lost a very dear woman friend she seemed quite unconsolable and I persuaded her to have a sitting with Mary Taylor. Mary described her friend in great detail and gave a series of very helpful messages from her. Then the medium said "Do you know a friend in Spirit who is named Stella?" My sister thought around her circle of friends and said "No, I don't think so." Mary was silent for a moment and then said "How very careless of me, it isn't a woman they are speaking of but a horse." My sister nearly jumped out of her chair, for if my great love is for monkeys, hers is for horses. "Why of course," she cried "My favourite mare was called Stella. We gave her that name because she had a white star on her forehead." My sister had always loved that horse and I think it cheered her quite as much to hear of Stella as did the messages from her friend. Mary told her that it was leading a very happy life in heavenly green pastures, beside still waters, but that whenever Kitty thought of it or spoke of it, it became as it were telepathically conscious of her and though maybe unseen, it came to her.

The next time I saw my sister, she said "Oh, Harold, I shall never forget that sitting! I would not have missed it for anything. Just to think that dear old Stella trots along to see me—isn't it wonderful."

Since then my sister quite suddenly 'slipped her moorings'. She left her physical body cold and stiff upon a hospital bed. It was buried beneath the trees in a Worcestershire Churchyard and flowers each season bloom on the grave —yet she is not there, of course. In the same green pastures where Stella lives overhung by graceful trees is the spiritual home where my sister lives. It is a mansion not built by hands—"nor with bricks and mortar but by kindly deeds done while on earth." With these my sister had builded her dwelling place. It is a record of the innumerable kindly deeds she performed while on earth. Some even thought she was foolishly kind. If so, all the same that life of kindness brought a rich reward of peace and joy. Her house is not too isolated, other of her friends in their 'dead houses' are quite near. When I have a sitting she often tells me of these friends and of all the cats, dogs and other animals—old favourites in her earth plane days, who still form part of her Heavenly family. They are all supremely happy together. In many ways it is like life upon Earth, only much lovelier and more peaceful.

I have a friend—a clergyman's widow, who as a child galloped all over the countryside on a favourite mare. People used to say that she was 'born' in the saddle, while reincarnationists declared that in a previous incarnation, she had been a skilled cavalryman. Whatever the explanation of her saddle consciousness, many years have passed since those childhood days. Yet from time to time, she is still as conscious of the spiritual nearness of her horse as she is of the physical nearness of the trees surrounding her house. She who in more orthodox days, before she had found the invisible key we have spoken of, might have laughed at the mere suggestion of animals surviving death, in her own experience now knows full well that they do.

Courtney Thorpe, a well-known actor in Victorian days, kept and loved a number of small dogs. He lived to be a great age, and although he had no fear of dying, was always very distressed as to what would happen to his dogs. He had arranged that a small legacy should be paid to a friend on condition that this friend 'adopted' his canine family.

Some years after his death an elderly woman came for a sitting. I saw clairvoyantly an old man surrounded by excited dogs jumping around him, and sometimes jumping around her. During the years, one by one they had left the home of their adoption, to bound forward through the invisible door to their original owner and friend who awaited them in the Spiritual realm. Now he was sending most grateful messages to his old housekeeper. I was told that while the dogs were still on the earth he almost haunted the woman's house where they were housed; but since they have gone to him in the spirit world, his presence is rarely felt.

Throughout the country what a number of shrines there are, dedicated to "Our Lady of Sorrows". How rarely a shrine to "Our Lady of Joy". But I did come across one, where people from far and near came to show thanks for their joys. I thought it a wonderful idea. It reminded me of the one grateful leper who returned to give thanks for his healing.

This shrine was decorated with sweet scented lilies when I first discovered it and I knelt there trying to count over the many joyous experiences I had had during my life and to express thanks. While I knelt an old man with a dog's collar and lead in his hand came and knelt by my side. His face was full of happiness. His lips moved as if in prayer. He knelt there for a long time and when he arose to go, I left the church and entered into conversation with him. And why do you think he had visited with thankfulness "Our Lady of Joy"? It appears he had for many years, a dog named Rover. It seemed almost as though they had grown together or become as roses may be—grafted. They did the shopping together in the morning, they dozed together in an afternoon and went for lovely long walks together if the evenings were fine. One afternoon, the old man's doze over, he spoke to the dog, but no response. Its body was there it is true, but there was no life in it. Life had liberated itself from so old and infirm a body. This had been a great shock to the old man. He grieved for weeks. Now for the first time he felt lonely.

Then, the day before I met him he had had a wonderfully revealing experience. He was awakened from his doze by the warm touch of a dog's tongue, licking his hand. He opened his eyes and for a brief moment he saw Rover. He was wagging his tail in a most natural manner. It was but a clairvoyant 'flash' but it was so real—so actual— he knew at once that it was no dream, no stretch of imagination. "Oh my God, I thank you for this revelation," he said with fervour, and it was this joy that had sent him to the shrine of "Our Lady of Joy". We found a seat in a quiet spot and talked long together of the Lordliness of Life and of the Nothingness of Death.

When people leave their home in one district and live in a fresh environment, maybe many miles away, animals can become quite a problem. They have become so accustomed to the old environment—they have their favourite walks and have found quiet spots for their afternoon nap where no one will disturb them, they have formed friendships and occasionally, I am afraid, the more human ones have made enemies too. And animals do not take easily to a strange abode. Very often they will retrace their steps travelling back many weary miles to the spot they have loved and 'made their own'. But since new people are in the old home and have their own four-legged family, the weary traveller is not welcome and becomes an outcast.

In our old village, however, fortunately from the animals' point of view, an old lady lived in a house which I think the animals must have called "Welcome Inn". Her cottage stood alone in a long quiet lane overhung by lordly elms and lordlier beeches. Its walled-in garden became an oasis of Love in a thoughtless world for all the lost, stolen or strayed creatures who came into the village. Dogs and cats, a parrot and a monkey and at one time a donkey and a goat. All were given a home and she loved them all without favouritism— as a mother loves her brood. She was a real protectress of the local animal world and woe betide the boy she caught with a catapult or the man with a rabbit-snare. She seemed to have a gift for teaching cats not to touch the birds, for her garden was almost an unwired aviary and all kinds of nests would be seen there. She and her husband were vegetarians and almost ageless for even the oldest inhabitants could remember calling her even in their younger days—"Old Mrs Usher!" Well of course, the time came (with her as it will with us) when she heard a Heavenly call— " Well done thou good and faithful servant, enter into thy reward," and the invisible door swung wide open, and to her new Home she hastened on.

At almost every sitting I have had, the medium, whoever it might be, would describe this dear old soul with her almost menagerie of lovely creatures; and further on I hope to tell you of how I too have passed through that invisible door and wandered by the side of a wise conductor to see something of that wonderful "Land that is Fairer than Day" and to tell of some of the old friends I have met there and how they are faring.

When I was six years old we had a dog named Hector. A big lumbering dog. It knocked me over many times and then would tug at my jacket trying to pull me up again. If he had been a man instead of a dog I fear that he might well have become a drunkard. I never knew a dog with such a thirst. He seemed to thrive on drinking. Every bucket of water, puddle of water, the water in the horses drinking troughs, dripping taps and if none of these were available he would pull at my mother's skirt and draw her towards the pump. Hector had been 'dead' for twenty years. I had almost forgotten his existence until one evening in a physical circle at the home of Glover Botham in Golders Green, Hector in full view of everybody, materialised. There was a large blue china bowl of water on the floor in the centre of the circle as this is thought sometimes to add power to aid the various manifestations. The materialised Hector, unmindful of the purpose for which the water was supplied, set to and very noisily lapped up the whole of it. Then he barked loudly as though to say "wasn't that clever." Later we heard that his bark had been heard by the two ladies living next door.

At about the same time I was at another séance when a lovely blue-green budgerigar materialised in a room which was in strong red light. There were eight people present. Gradually a blue-green mist began to move over the sitters heads and from this ectoplasmic formation there flew a budgerigar. It circled around the room then settled on a man's shoulder. He had owned the bird two years previously but it had been 'killed' by a cat. It evidently recognised its owner for in a very clear voice—as though appealing to him—it said "I want a cigarette." This made everyone laugh. It appears that its owner was a chain smoker and had so often made this remark that the budgie had learned to mimic him.

Some animals have a very strong magnetic influence and that is why some mediums allow their dogs or cats to be present during a séance, as, to use the common phrase, "they give power" and this can make a great contribution to the success of the séance. This may well be so.

I have a friend who owns a farm deep in the country. She milks her cows in the cow-shed and undoubtedly that building is full of psychic power. She had often told me that she receives more inspiration and sees lovelier visions there than anywhere else. I can quite believe it. In the busy rush of life—as we have made it—and "when the heart is full of din" and cares cast a dark shadow on every hand and hasty words fly around, the atmosphere is too disturbed for communion with a finer sphere. In her cow shed, surrounded by the cows she loves—and make no mistake about it, they love her too—there is peace!—a "peace that passeth understanding". In such an atmosphere it is as though the two worlds draw nearer. Then she becomes conscious of the nearness of her Father and Mother—long passed to the Fairer Land; and in the daily perplexities, their presence inspires courage and their counsel illumines her pathway with light. Most people perhaps would not call this cow-shed a sanctuary—yet twice daily she is there in sweet communion with angels and archangels.

The sweet-scented hay is the incense even as it was long ago in the lowly cattle shed at Bethlehem. It is there that she realises that behind the material scenes "the shuttles of unseen powers" are working. It is there that in ecstasy she realises the immense majesty of Nature's God who is the Father of beast and bird and human kind and who is the Great Giver of all. In her spiritual joy in this Holy of Holies she might almost have composed a lovely hymn they sing in Sweden, which pays tribute to the Giver of all, and warns not to be forgetful of his bounty. I am afraid I translate it inadequately :

"I cannot count them all—
The proofs of God's bounty I've received
Like dewdrops in the morning they glitter
And glimmer as beautiful as these.

Like the numberless hosts of the stars
They neither have number nor name
But like these they ever shine brightly
Even in my darkest valley.

I cannot count them all
But let me not forget one with my thanks
What wonders of Love He showers
Yea Love He outpours upon all."

Some years ago I knew an elderly woman who in her earlier years had hoped to become a nun. She had entered a convent as novice, but after three years her health broke down and she returned to the world of men and women. She loved "all creatures great and small " and stories of her many kindnesses both to man and beast spread far and wide. Indeed her life became—as someone once said—"a living rosary where each bead was a good deed." I have always been grateful that she taught me her favourite prayer:

"O Immortal Essence, under various forms manifesting, enable me to reverence all life since it is of Thee. Help me that I hurt no thing which Thou hast made for it is Thine and Thy Love enfoldeth it."

She used to say that the earth was a mystical workshop in which mankind was creating everlasting character; and that love poured forth, whether to man or beast, was the greatest beautifier of the work in hand blessing both him who gives and him who receives. I had been to her home for tea one Sunday and afterwards we were sitting on a seat in the garden talking of the things of the Spirit, oblivious to the second-by-second passing of time. It was already twilight and trees and shrubs cast deep shadows, yet gay nasturtiums gleamed here and there and tall hollyhocks stood like a group of tall guardsmen near the gate. Sometimes, even where a group of people are talking, a sudden silence falls and someone says "an angel is passing." Such a silence interrupted our conversation as we sat—a hushed silence. Then we both saw it—a lovely golden retriever trotting towards us on the pathway between the rhododendrons—a magnificent dog. "It is Nebo," my friend explained, "I'm pleased you saw him. It isn't everyone who does." It had already vanished from mortal sight but we were both sure that it was still there. Only for a moment or two—yet the memory of that vision is still quite clear. "There," said my friend "Isn't that a proof that Death is but the gate to Life Immortal for animals as well as for humans. How I wished that all my friends realised it." Then she told me that many of her 'arisen' friends have from time to time become visible to her in her garden.

She was not a Spiritualist and would perhaps have been annoyed if anyone had called her one, but from early childhood she had been psychic and though she would no doubt have shuddered at the word, her garden was in reality her séance room. She brought the right conditions into a place which oozed peace. It was a garden of material beauty it is true but it was to her, I'm sure, also a garden of the soul where Heaven's wonderful workings would be registered and the deep things of the spirit revealed. There came at length, a day when people gathered in gossiping groups and said of her, "She is dead." How lacking in understanding. It was only the body she had discarded that was lifeless. She was already radiantly happy in a realm of pure delight—not far removed from earth—only one wave-length away; and she was re-united in the re-established companionship of those who had gone before. And you may be sure Nebo's tail would wag a wonderful welcome.

Doctor James Tyler Kent, a man of great wisdom, once wrote: "We're all encumbered by tradition. The tendency to ridicule what we do not understand is born within us." I was reminded of this saying of his when a friend 'died' who loved the wild birds—indeed all wild life. Instead of erecting the conventional gravestone I asked the vicar of the parish if I could place at the grave, as a memorial, a marble bird-bath with a carved inscription:

> " All things great and small,
> The Lord God made them all."

He was most indignant and refusing said, " It would lead to all sorts of wrong ideas." "That is not my wish," I said, "I hoped that it would lead to all sorts of right ideas, and I am sure it would be very acceptable to the one in whose memory it was created." But this very orthodox vicar thought that as animals have no souls, the 'faithful' in Heaven would cease to be interested in them; and in any case it might induce ignorant people on earth to think that animals in God's sight were as important as humans. A few years afterwards he 'died', and I have often thought how surprised he must have been to discover in the Heavenly Courts that the text he must have frequently read—"Not one sparrow falleth to the ground but your Heavenly Father careth," was no mere platitude. How shocked he must have been to find there, not only sparrows, but dogs and donkeys and indeed all the animals, poor Adam—if tradition is reliable—had the unenviable job of naming, survive.

Talking of sparrows reminds me of another survival incident. I had been very friendly for many years with two suffragettes who lived together in Lancaster Gate. They were both great animal lovers. One day they found a sparrow with a broken wing. With great care and with the aid of matchsticks they set the wing and nursed the bird back to health. It fed from their hands and became so tame that at length when they tried to persuade it to fly off to rejoin its mates it refused to leave them. They named it "Spadgey" and it seemed quite at home and happy with a Georgian drawing room as its cage. At night, it adopted a niche in a carved oak overmantle where it slept quite soundly until the morning. Although the windows were open daily it never attempted to fly away. Occasionally it would hop on to the ledge outside the window, have a peep around—looking this way and that way but no doubt thinking that the way of the world outside with its noise and rushing confusion was no place for a self-respecting sparrow—it was much cosier in the drawing room. Sometimes, especially when he caught sight of his reflection in the mirror, he would chatter very noisily but generally he chirped quite softly as though talking to himself.

They loved it. From time to time it would settle on their shoulders and very softly chatter to them as though confiding to them some deep secret. My friends would answer "Really," and "Is that so," and this would encourage "Spadgey" to elaborate his theme with many a wise nod and twist of the head. It was most amusing and I am sure that "Spadgey" enjoyed it as much as the rest. Then the day came after three years, when for some never discovered reason he flew from his feathered earthly body and from his devoted earthly friends to the haven of all sparrows who enter the Invisible spheres. Oh how we all missed him. He has frequently been seen clairvoyantly, and since the good ladies who nursed him back to health have passed to the Spirit World, they too have returned with him. I have seen them myself, and several other mediums have seen them and described them to me.

A woman came for a sitting some time ago. First of all, her husband spoke of personal affairs and then he said, "Tell my wife that I have got our neighbour's old dog with me. She will be pleased." I passed on the message and then the sitter told me this—"For more than two years my husband was a very sick man and in great pain, in good weather he would sit on the lawn in a deck chair—he loved the open air. We had no dog but the neighbour next door had one which they had bought as a deterrent against burglars. They fed it it is true, but they had no love for it. It was just a commodity. My husband used to be very sorry for it and no doubt it could sense his sympathy. Soon a hole began to appear in the boundary hedge. It became larger and larger until it was large enough for the dog to come through. It became a wonderful companion to my husband. It came daily and gave him untold pleasure. But the neighbour to whom it belonged was so jealous because his dog was happier with my husband in our garden than in his that one day in a fit of temper he shot it. He could not have done anything more unkind. My husband cried like a heartbroken child. I have not seen a medium before, but it is wonderful that my husband has the dog. It makes me very happy to know that, for I am sure they will be happy together."

Sometimes this little understood psychic faculty in man kind asserts its power suddenly in a person who has previously had no such experiences and who might have been incredulous if anyone else had told them of their experiences.

In our village there lived an old man who very many years before had fought under Kitchener at Khartoum. And many were the tales he told of his adventures there. The village boys loved to sit in his kitchen and hear the stories he could tell. "Tell us some more," they would say and I am sure they must have heard the same stories over and over again through the years but that did not matter, it was all helping to pass the evening, and the old man had a remarkably descriptive gift. He had a dog. I never knew its

28

name. He always alluded to it as "The old bitch". "Open the door, Harold please, the old bitch wants to come in" and such like.

I had been living in London for some years and felt that I needed a dose of native air. So I went to the old village home for a holiday and, of course, went down to see the old soldier. "I hear you have taken up with Spiritualism," he said. "Yes," I replied, "a very interesting subject." "Well now—do you mind if I tell you something?" he asked. "Something I daren't tell anyone in this place. If I did they would think that I was about ready for the asylum." And then he told me this: "One day I had been setting potatoes in the field all morning. At dinner time, I came in to my cottage to put a saucepan of stew on the fire to heat up and as my back ached I lay down on my couch till my dinner should be hot. All at once it seemed as though the kitchen wall faded away and in its place was a great open window looking on to a wonderful green lawn. On the lawn stood a round table with a lovely crochet table cloth on it. There were various chairs stood about. My father and my mother and my aunt sat on three of them and my old bitch (you remember her— I had her when I first came to live here, she has now been dead for it couple of years or more), lay at my mother's feet.

Presently, I heard my mother say to my father—"I wonder if Tom will have a rough passage," (meaning my brother Tom in Ireland). Hardly had my mother finished speaking, than our Tom came along with his characteristic swing, kissed them all, and the old bitch jumped around him as though pleased to welcome him (it was Tom who gave me the bitch when he had decided to go to Dublin). Naturally I was so astonished at all this but before you could say Jack Robinson the kitchen wall was back and the lawn and the family gone. Two days later, I heard that Tom had had a stroke as he was having his dinner and died before he gained consciousness. All those on the lawn—including the old bitch, were dead, so I think there must be something in your Spiritualism, but for the Lord's sake don't breathe a word in the village while I live here for you know what they are."

The old man has passed on now. He has joined his family on their lawn just as naturally as did Tom, and I am sure the old bitch was delighted to welcome him for, in his rough way, he was very fond of her. At his funeral the village lads brought simple bunches of flowers from their cottage gardens with sprays of sweet smelling lads-love and honeysuckle—but he was not there, the coffin contained but the material he had finished with. I am reminded of the woman in the gospel story setting forth to a grave with sweet smelling spices, yet He for Whom the sweet spices were brought was walking in spirit in the dew drenched garden.

I stayed for a holiday in a country cottage facing a field of golden corn, very generously riddled with scarlet wild poppies. The cottage came almost flush to the roadside, there was no pavement—just road—then the doorstep, but rich compensation was at the back—such a long garden and at the end, a small orchard of apple trees. On a large slab of stone in this orchard was carved a simple inscription—"Our Nell." It appears that the owner some years earlier found a collarless lost dog. They tried to discover the owner without success, so Nell became their property. "She was absolutely without any vice," my host told me over and over again. Sunday walks were its great joy for then Nell and her master wandered together through fields and woods and quiet country lanes.

"She knew Sunday as well as she knew her own kennel," he said. He had little time for walks on weekdays but wet or fine, Sunday was Nell's day. She knew every rabbit-hole and the drains where rats had been. Occasionally, she pricked up her ears if she heard a dog bark in the distance but never had she been known to quarrel or to fight. Very rarely did she venture on to the main road alone—but one day—her last day on earth, she trotted on to the road, just as a swiftly driven car was approaching. Death was instantaneous. She is happy now in the fields and lanes of Heaven wondering in her doggy way when her master will come Home to share her walks. Only her body is buried in the orchard. But when in that cottage home they talk of her, she pricks up her ears and crosses the barrier and sits with them, docile as ever, but, of course, unseen by them. It was when they were telling me of her that I first saw her. What a lovely creature. I told them of her presence, but you know I do not think they quite believed me. However, when they eventually go to where she has gone they will realise that Life cannot die. Each fragment of it is part of the limitless Kingdom of God.

Father Adderley of Birmingham once described man as a "sordid gold-seeker", well, if such sordid fragments survive, why not Nell? And if Nell, why not the lovely creature you have lost?

Nancy Cunard as a child had a pretty little Shetland pony. She was very fond of it and talked to it as she would have talked to you or me. And what is more, judging by the looks of it, you would have said it understood every word. Her parents were far too occupied with their own interests to pay a great deal of attention to Nancy so she was handed into the care of a strict (and Nancy thought) somewhat sadistic governess. Whenever she could escape she found her way to the stables and to the stall where her pony lived. To it she confided all her woes, and when pleasures came along as they sometimes did, her pleasures also. Scripture says:

> "Rejoice with those who do rejoice
> and weep with those who weep."

It really seemed as though the pony did just that. At any rate, Nancy thought so, and her grief was great when at last the pony died. She felt that she had indeed lost a friend.

To all of us, I think, this earthly life seems a strange mixture of riddles not too easy to solve. We often have to grope in the dark a long time before we find a light. The road we choose does not always lead to where we think it should. Yet through it all character is being built; though only as we are nearing the end of the journey and looking backwards over the zig-zag route we have taken, do we see something of the pattern of it all, and "in the quiet pastures of the mind" it is borne upon us that beyond the gateway of this world of confusion is the realm where " to know all is to forgive all." Nancy with many adventurous years to her credit, passed. And within days visited my séance room and told me that the first thing that caught her eye as she entered the Finer Realm, was Bert, her stable boy of many years ago leading, to greet her, her dear old Shetland pony. She had never quite realised to how great a degree "The Love of God" is broader than the measures of man's mind. For it was He who designed the Hereafter and He has made all things well. Looking at our civilisation we could sometimes wonder if that is true until we realise that we—not He— made our civilisation what it is—very largely in defiance of His Will.

At the Church of the Good Shepherd (what a lovely name) in London each month, a service was held for the healing of sick animals and I frequently attended and saw some wonderful results. All kinds of animals and birds were brought. One Sunday, a young gipsy brought his tame raven—and being interested in gipsy life—(a life so much misunderstood) and so fascinated by ravens, I spoke to the youth after the service. He had had Jacko for two years and it was rarely out of his sight, but one day it disappeared. He spent a long time looking for it but to no avail—but one day it hobbled home with a broken leg. He thought it might have settled on a trap or caught his leg in a snare. He had patched the leg up as well as he could with a plaster of comfrey-root overlaid with elastoplast, but having heard of the Good Shepherd healing sessions he came all the way from Maidenhead, well armed with hope which is perhaps the next best thing to faith. "You never know," he had said to his companion, "I have said 'Good God' many a time when I have been ruffled but perhaps I spoke the truth without knowing it. At any rate I will try anything once." And I am glad to report that the bird's leg was cured.

For some years, I kept in touch with him and occasionally he brought Jacko around to see me. The bird loved all bright and glittering objects and if given one would immediately hide it under a book or saucer or if outdoors—a leaf or stone. Sixpences were his great delight for they were easy for him to handle and he would run about with it in his beak. He looked most quaint. When he found a safe hiding place he would slyly slide it out of sight then turn round challengingly as though to say "now touch that if you dare." If one pretended to retrieve the hidden coin, with wings outstretched and beak wide open

33

he would pretend to be most furious and all sorts of bird swear words came forth. But it was only a show—part of the game. He would stand guard over his treasure for an hour if need be. It had been given to him and he wasn't going to part with it.

Three or four years more passed and the gipsy youth was now a fine man. One day when he called, I said "And how is Jacko?" "Ah poor Jacko was shot," he replied. "Some farmer not knowing that it was a tame bird, thinking it might be after his corn, let fly and it was killed as dead as a door-nail." He said it sadly but with an air of fatalism.

"Well you know," I said "it isn't as dead as a door-nail—it is still living a very fine life in a realm where farmers do not carry shot guns—and you will realise it one day." We had tea—one of those movable feasts, early or late, it is a pleasant social occasion—and we talked. He asked me what made me think that Jacko still lived, and then I told him some of the things I have been telling you. Perhaps he was not quite convinced—I certainly think it needs personal experience to be absolutely sure about it all. " You experienced the Power of the Spirit at the Church of The Good Shepherd," I remarked "It is that same Spiritual Power which makes the whole Universe tick—both the seen and the unseen. Life Force is within everything which lives and it responds to what I can only call an External Life Force. Jacko was the name you gave to a fragment of life manifesting in a feathered body. The feathered body by the very nature of things will disintegrate and become a rotting mass just as will a human body in time but the fragment of life will be liberated. That cannot die for life is everlasting. The life you called Jacko can never be destroyed—only the husk that enshrouded Jacko. Your life can never be destroyed, though one day your body will be either cremated or buried. You will still, however, be living in a far more wonderful realm than this and perhaps be astonished to find that Jacko spots your arrival and greets you very joyously."

We talked, or perhaps I ought to say, I talked. He was a good listener. Perplexed, but with great trust in me, he accepted as much as he could. Later I hope to tell you how at length he knew beyond peradventure how everlasting is Life and how fragmentary is its period on earth —but that was not until he had passed through the gate of God's Celestial Garden. Presently, I will tell you of how he fared there but first I want to tell you another incident about another animal—a little cat. I have so often told the first part of that story but not the ending. I had not then known the ending.

My sister had a cat, a smokey-black one. I think she loved it more than any of the others—there were four—then one day it was missing. It did not return at night and my sister became frantic when nearly a week went by with no news. An advertisement was telephoned to the local paper giving minute descriptions—its height, its colour, its name and its particularly wide face, etc., etc. Letters came from miles around. Everyone seemed to have found missing cats. She dashed hither and thither, her last searching spot turned out to be a fried fish shop. A stray had walked into the shop some days earlier—had adopted the fishy smelling shop—but the proprietor, being a keen business man, did not want a cat on the premises to eat up all the profits. "No, that is not my pussy," said my sister. "Well then, I shall have to drown it," said the man, probably sensing what the reaction would be. "Oh you cannot drown it," said my sister. "It is a beautiful little thing. It would be a crime to drown it." They argued for some little time then my sister said, "Well, I think my puss must be dead. I will have this kitten to replace him," and she bought it. She took it home, fed it well and it became a lovely cat.

One day it was on the garden seat playing with the other cats. "Oh, they look so pretty," she said, and she ran and brought her camera and snapped. When the film was developed the head of the missing Tommy was joined to Blackie so that Blackie appeared to have two heads. This is an excellent psychic photograph, taken by an amateur in broad daylight. There is no mistaking the broad face of Tommy against the more normal shape and truer black of Blackie.

One more cat anecdote. Very many years ago when I was only newly interested in Spiritualism, I used to visit each Saturday evening a house in Golders Green where four or five of us sat regularly at a little round table, for what was called a 'table-sitting'. Willie Baldwin, the son of the owner of the house, was in the Spirit World and he was mostly the communicator. He was able to rap out messages in code quite quickly and quite clearly. One evening towards the end of the session the rapping spelled out "Tell Harold to rescue the perishing—even the little one has an important part to play in destiny." We did not know what this meant and though we asked, no reply came forth as the power had waned. When the séance was over our hostess, as usual, brought in tea and cakes and we had a sort of social evening. When we opened the door to go to our various homes, a blizzard was blowing and snow whirled in to the passage. But on the doorstep was a tiny

36

cat looking lost and very forlorn. I recognised it at once as a cat I had often spoken to as it sat on its garden gate near my own home two miles away. "Here is the solution to the mystery," I said, "Here is the perishing creature which had to be rescued," and off I set with it as comfortable as I could make it under my top coat.

When I arrived at the right door I rang the bell and eventually—from his bed, a man came in his dressing gown. "I believe this is your cat," I said "I found it in Golders Green." The man was very curious as to how I knew it and where I had found it and out came the story of the table sitting and the message. He invited me in, put on an electric fire and we talked till the early hours. His was a sad story. Within a very short period, his wife, his mother and now his boy had passed to Spirit leaving him a lonely and dejected man. Now, for days, even his cat has been missing. When I told him about the séance, he said "I know nothing about Spiritualism, but I need something to give me a grip on life again, would it be possible for me to go to one of these séances do you think?" Shortly after, Helen Duncan was to hold a séance in Golders Green. I took the bereaved man—a picture of desolation when we went, but at the end of the evening he said "Let us walk home if you don't mind, I feel as though I shall walk on air—I cannot get over it. It was too wonderful for words." For his son had materialised and kissed him and brought messages from his wife and his mother who promised to materialise another time. During the experience of one short evening he could have written in his diary—"From sadness unto gladness." Truly the little cat had played an important part in destiny. In time that man discovered his own psychic gift and under the care and guidance of an experienced medium was able to develop his own 'receiving set' and to link once every week in, what was to him, a holy hour with his loved ones; and what a difference it made to his life.

It has often been said by people ignorant of the subject that it is wrong to communicate with the Spirit World. But surely God is the Creator of all the Laws of Life and if there is a Law by which the two realms may make contact, then it is God who made the Law, and since He is the "Great Wisdom" He can only have formed that Law in order that it might be used. He would not be likely as "The Great Wisdom" to say "I have made a Law but for the Lord's sake do not use it." It is a Law that enables the mourner to mourn no more, for she has found comfort and realises that Love is not broken by 'death'.

For some years I was in charge of a healing clinic at The Spiritualist Association of Great Britain in Belgrave Square. Generally, the sick were human beings, of course, but we had, from time to time, sick animals in our clinic and they responded to the healing power just as well as did the human beings. I remember particularly, a dog which used to have epileptic fits—"Do not touch him," said his owner, "He does not like strangers." You see, the dog's owner did not know what we know about that orange ray. Never grab at a dog or make a sudden move towards it until it has had time to sense your radiance. Then fearlessly put out the hand palm upward. It will perhaps seem to you that it is smelling your fingers. No—its nose is a sensitive machine. It is interpreting you. As soon as it has 'weighed you up' and finds that your intention is good, proceed. I did just that and the healing rays did the rest. He came for several weeks and not only did its fits cease but that snappy nervousness, which had made its owner fearful lest it should bite me, was overcome.

I remember being called to a farmer's cow. It had a nasty ulcer on its udder and was in great discomfort. Again the farmer warned me to be careful as it would resent my touching it. Be it remembered that rays are rays. They go forth like beams of light and energy. Although healing is usually by contact of the hand, when there is intense inflammation even a light pressure may cause greater pain. In such cases I hold my hand about an inch from the sore and watch the inflammation wane. I did that with the cow. Talking to it in sympathetic tones I calmed its fear. It was fastened to its stall, but it turned its head and looked me up and down.

Sitting on the stool the farmer used for milking, I placed my hands so that the tips of the fingers of both hands were directly over the ulcer. The cow stood wonderfully still. I sat in this manner for about twenty minutes. The ulcer and around was an angry blue when I started operations, now it was but a pale red. We adjourned, had a walk around the farm and in a couple of hours the same treatment was resumed. I wasn't able to give further treatments as I was due on the following day to journey to Edinburgh, but the farmer reported that "Old Bess never looked back after treatment."

I have mentioned the above about the healing rays for if your pets are in pain and there is neither healer nor vet at hand, you will know what to do. In faith stretch out your hand and Heaven's Power will unite with your own to bless and to heal. Long ago there was a Carpenter's Son, who was a great Healer. Some of His friends were astonished at the seemingly miraculous cures wrought by Him but He

39

answered their astonishment by saying the things which I can do, ye can do. And I am sure that is so of every generation. It is when people have no faith in their own powers—in the fact that this healing gift has been universally passed on—that they fear to attempt. Mankind is endowed with far greater powers than he realises.

I have talked a great deal about the Great Spiritual Realm—but have I seen it? Part of it, yes. Most people when they are tired go to bed and sleep. While their body and their brain are resting it frequently happens that their spirit travels far from the limitations of the flesh, for the Spirit is quite adventurous and has wonderful powers. Though still attached by a tenuous cord to the body, it can wander far over the Earth or far through the spheres at will. This spirit journeying is called astral travelling and I believe that from time to time everyone experiences this, though they may remember nothing of it upon waking. This is quite understandable, for the brain, which registers our deeds, is sleeping and the fantastic experiences of the spiritual flights are not generally registered, though they may sometimes be recorded quite clearly.

I remember Sir Arthur Conan Doyle recounting an instance of astral travel. He was away from home at the time and a man in deep sleep, a complete stranger, afterwards told him that he had just returned from Sir Arthur's house where he had seen Lady Doyle sitting in her room reading a book. He told Doyle the title of the book and described its cover and the exact position in which Lady Doyle was sitting. When Sir Arthur reached home, he asked Lady Doyle what she was doing at that time and it proved to be precisely the same as the stranger had described.

At about the same time another friend told me that he had an invitation to visit a Religious Community in Mirfield in Yorkshire. He had never been in Yorkshire but on the night before he was to travel there, he awoke suddenly with a clear picture of the house he was to visit and of the Superior of the Community. When he arrived there on the following day, both the house and the Superior were exactly as he remembered from his astral visitation.

When I was living in Hampstead, I set aside one night each week for a circle of friends to sit with me, that we might train ourselves to travel together astrally and to bring back clear memories of what we had seen while "absent from the body" as St. Paul called it. There were twelve of us. It needed great patience. For a year there were veriest fragments, but as we learned how to be thoroughly quiescent, more and more clearly registrations were made. At first our journeyings were almost always to some earthly scene, but as we progressed we were able to travel through the Spiritual Spheres. No wonder the hymn writer coined the phrase, "There's a Land that is Fairer than Day." For many years that circle sat, the same twelve, with such loyalty and devotion. Only sickness kept anyone away.

'Out of the body' we have travelled the Heavens. Spiritual Guides were with us ever ready with suggestions and explanations. Generally speaking we all went together and came back together—away for maybe an hour in what I could only call bliss. No wonder we have no fear of death—no wonder we say "They are not dead,"—these citizens of Heaven. No wonder we can say to the animal lover, "You will find them waiting for you." Our knowledge has not been gleaned from books, we have seen. The war service call broke up the circle to a great extent and some of the sitters have now become inhabitants of those wonderful realms, but we few who are left behind for a while still journey forward, while our bodies sleep, and bring back happy memories .

What are these Spiritual Realms like? You remember that I said that all life survives. Did you know that even rock contains the essence of life just as surely as you do? Thus as we travelled we saw wonderful mountains and forests, gentle hills and valleys, rippling rivers and quiet streams, green fields and colourful gardens, much as a traveller would on earth—only more so. Such colours, I never saw on earth—nor such grandeur. Nor elsewhere have I felt such peace and joy. On one occasion Brother Peter said "Come this way, I would like you to meet an old friend." He led through a larch wood. There was thick moss on the path and in a clearing stood a very colourful caravan, on the steps of which sat my gipsy friend with his raven and a couple of dogs which I had not met before. What a lot he had to tell me about his new life and how day by day he was understanding more and more how life is governed by a wonderful Law. His guide came forward, a Spanish gipsy, who had lived on Earth in the Middle Ages. My friend, during all his earth life had had no idea that step by step with him in all his difficulties and sorrows, there went this Companion, encouraging, uplifting. The raven—Jacko—evidently remembered me because he flew onto my shoulder and chattered as though to say "Hail fellow, well met."

While we were talking a young boy of about twelve came along with a tame rabbit in his arms. He told me that his name was Jim and that his rabbit was called Billy. He and the gipsy were great pals on Earth and they had found each other as was quite natural in those fields of larger life.

While we were talking the strains of a piano and violin sounded. I turned to Brother Peter and said "Surely there are not pianos in Heaven." He smiled and said "Do you still think there are only harps?" He suggested that we should go further and see who was playing. Our path lay through a denser wood, then among handsome beech trees till we entered a clearing at the end of which stood a cottage.

The door was wide open and on the grass outside was a perfect menagerie of animals. Through the open door we could see from whence the music came, Mrs Usher and her husband Dan. How pleased I was to see them. Piano and violin were laid aside and what a confabulation we had in which Brother Peter and the Guides of their household joined. They were the good, kind souls who rescued all the stray and unwanted animals in our village so long ago. They looked younger and more vital than ever and the animals, without which the Ushers would not have been complete, were playing about in absolute freedom, not even a garden wall to hem them in. That was a thing that struck me more and more in my heavenly visits—no boundaries, no fences, no "trespassers prosecuted" notices. One was free to wander everywhere. The inhabitants spoke of "our world" not of "my property". Their houses and dwellings were their own, of course, for they, by their deeds, had built them, but there seemed to be no possessiveness, no pride in ownership. I am sure everyone who felt 'drawn' there would be welcomed as a neighbour in anyone's house for the feeling of magnetic harmony is very real and one only seems to meet those who are attuned to the same key.

On the way back in a luscious green field on a kind of knoll sat an old shepherd I had known as a boy. His crook was by his side as he watched his flock of sheep. "What, shepherding here?" I asked him. He replied, "Ah lad, I would never be happy without my sheep, we know each other so," and a couple of lambs bleated as though to say "I quite agree."

But it must not be supposed that only English folk survive and only English animals and birds. Further afield I found lions and tigers, foxes, elephants, monkeys and meditative camels, and tropical birds of brilliant colour. Indeed, every living creature you could think of. The prophesy that the lion should lie down with the lamb was no fable. In this Land without fear, harming instincts seemed to be non-existent. Groups of people—many of whom on earth lived in distant lands, were strolling in friendly groups and there were children of every shade and colour romping in childish glee playing games in which the wild animals often joined. I remember one lady evidently newly arrived from Earth excitedly crying "Look Elsie, that lion has actually licked my feet."

On one occasion I saw a man in a long cream-coloured robe. At first I thought he might be a monk, but Brother Peter told me that he was a teacher from a higher sphere. He began talking from a kind of open air pulpit and soon numbers of people were gathering around to hear. There was no compulsion, people came if they wished to hear. His discourse was of service and it embraced service to the earthly dweller, to the newly arrived citizens who might feel strange where ideals were actually put into practice. Service to the animals and birds especially to those who had been brutally slaughtered and who came hither, still panicing with fear. It could not have been more simple or more inspiring. There was no rhetoric, no gesticulation. It was Love, inviting the dwellers in Love, to love doing for others. To go about even in the Land of Happiness, like the Carpenter's Son of old, 'doing good'. One of his remarks I remember quite well—"When you desire to serve, your power which may be little is infused by a mighty power and the influx makes the little to do mightily."

When he had gone, Brother Peter told me that when on Earth this man had lived in Palestine and had been a worker in a baker's shop, and that once he had been sent with his wares to sell to a crowd of people gathered on a mountain slope but on the way so many people bought his wares that by the time he reached the crowd there was very little left to sell. But the One whose words were influencing the people to have Faith in Him to whom nothing is impossible—God, the Father of all mankind—called him, blessed the food within the basket, and said to his friends "Feed them all," and somehow the food, scanty as it had seemed, was sufficient to satisfy everyone. Faith, Service, plus the inflow of the Mighty Power did the seemingly impossible.

On another occasion I went with Brother Peter to a wonderful swimming pool. It was near the Gateway from Earth and when people or animals come over in great fear they are encouraged to swim, and so soothing are the waters that fear memories fade. This pool was surrounded by hawthorn trees in full flower and the perfume itself was soothing. Sitting on a bank, it was here that we heard many stories of fears conquered. Four friends and their dog had been killed in a motor car accident. The horror at the moment of impact was terrific but almost instantly as they came through the Great Doorway, they were asked— "Would you like a refreshing bath? It will do you good." And immediately the shock was taken from them.

Another young man had committed suicide. He had been beset by fears over wrongs that he had done and had felt that the only relief could come in ending his life. Little did he realise that Life never ends. He was taken aside after his bathing by a Wise One who talked and soothed and showed a way of service open to him.

Later, on another visit to the same sphere, I met this man again—now very happy for he had found a wonderful vocation in learning how to contact fearful and unhappy earth dwellers who were contemplating suicide and persuading them not to do so, and he had had much success and this naturally made him very happy.


I have mentioned some of the special animal friends and pets of people, but what about the millions of wild animals who had never been owned or loved by anyone? Well, there is a wonderful zone where they abide in perfect freedom. They are not fenced in and are quite free to come to the zone where men and women of the Grand World live but they love the wildness of their sphere. It is home to them. Brother Peter and a wise woman who had always loved animals took me. Although English by birth, she had lived in Persia for some years and had all through a long life tried to inspire people to a love of animals. She had sowed many seeds but had seen but a scant harvest when she was on the Earth. But no sooner had she reached the heavens than she heard a voice crying "Welcome— Come, you are wanted in the animal sphere," and there to her amazement she found animals she had rescued from cruel homes. Animals she had prayed for, and, would you believe it, the little brown squirrel she had rescued from the murderous clutches of a cannibalistic grey squirrel.

"Will you help us to make the wild beasts happy?" they asked her and no task could have given her greater joy. What a wonderful journey that was—"Birds and Beasts and Insects bright" all the way. Trees and bushes and grasses and mosses of every description from the pines of Scotland to the palms of the tropics. Glades and thickets and sunny clearings, lakes and rivers and cascades making rippling music. Our Guide's name was Laura. "What animals do you most like?" she asked. "Monkeys," I replied. "Wait a moment," she said. We stood still. She did not audibly call but she concentrated, and in a very short time, monkeys bounded towards us. They were friendly and, of course, full of curiosity. Laura concentrated again and a wise old capuchin jumped on to my shoulder lightly and lovingly. Then a gibbon took hold of Brother Peter's hand and so we went forward. Conversation with the animals seemed to be through concentration. Laura's thoughts reached them and they obeyed. Asked if she could call others in a like manner, she replied "Certainly, what shall I call?" I asked for an elephant and a camel. And lo and behold, a velvety elephant plodded towards us and slightly behind him a lovely old camel. No load was now on his back, he was more free than any earth plane dweller.

"Come and see them as they are in their inner zone," she said. "I do not call them from there, they come and go openly at their own desire. I only call those who are wandering in their outer zone." We climbed a hill and saw below a sunlit valley, woods and copses and a wide ribbon of water. It stretched for unnumbered miles. We talked as we descended into the valley. Indeed it was a valley of peace. Lovely creatures, many of whom had learned in a sad school to fear and to hate man for his cruelty. Some had been hunted to death, some trapped in steel traps, but here was peace. And only those humans who radiated love and pity and compassion and mercy, were allowed within the valley. Deer, tigers, rabbits, wolves, foxes, badgers, lions, apes, squirrels, field mice, horses and ponies, such as one sees on Dartmoor, and lots more. We walked among them and because of our radiation, none were afraid. "It is here that they can live perfectly natural lives," said Laura. "Waking or sleeping, exercising or resting, just as they please. It is their Heaven. These are the once wild beasts so called. But would you like to go to the zone where peoples' pets live who have come to the Happy Land."

Laura concentrated again and presently there came along two young men. They seemed to know what was wanted. "Will you come this way?" the elder one said. "For I see you are animal lovers." "How do you know?" I asked. "You are wearing the animal lovers' colour," he replied smiling. "We know very much about a person as soon as we see their aura." The younger man hurried ahead to a clearing among the trees and he called softly. To my astonishment there came forth two of the late members of my circle—both great animal lovers—what welcoming greetings they gave me.

"Isn't it wonderful, we are all among the animals giving them love and care until the one who owned them shall come from earth." And then I discovered that animals that have been greatly loved on earth draw to themselves people who will love them and to whom they can give love until their own owners come. This zone was rather more like an English countryside—fields and houses, and all the houses were lived in by animal lovers. They had gravitated as it were to the right spot. Theirs was a mission of mercy, yet a mission they enjoyed. This zone also stretched for countless miles and through the fields, and in the lanes people were romping with dogs, and in their homes fondling cats or talking to birds which needed no cages because they do not fly away from love.

The sceptic may say in scorn "What a Heaven!" I reply, "Is it worse than a throne-room filled with harp players?" It is a Good Heaven. It was planned—like all things—by Him whose Love is broader than the measures of man's mind, and the Heart of the Eternal is most wonderfully kind. When I was telling a little boy about the animal spheres much as I have been telling you, he said "Mr. Sharp, God seems to have thought of everything, hasn't He?" You know, we are blind to so much. We concentrate so completely upon the outside of things. We close our ears to the whisperings of angels and we make a stranger of the Divine Essence. It is in that Heavenly Realm that the eyes of the blind are opened and the ears of the deaf unstopped. "The Eternal Loveliness" and "The Harmony of the Spheres" are not exaggerated phrases. Do not think that Heaven is only filled with animal lovers and their pets and the wilder creatures of life. I have concentrated upon these as you are so sad when your pets go to Paradise to be wonderfully happy—even happier than you can make them. But like you, they have a memory and they have loyalty, and the moment you pass through the Doorway, they will be by your side. It is always so. You are no exception—God has thought of everything.

Indeed some of His Essence is in them, even as some of His Essence is in you. Do you remember a hymn which says:

"*To all* Life Thou givest to both great and small
*In all Life* Thou livest, the true life of all."

49

I have stressed certain words in the hymn as I think that makes the meaning of the writer more clear. We often say that all human beings are the children of God because His Essence is within them. That is true but His Essence is in all living things. No one created Life, but Him, and His Essence being in all living things makes all living things related. That is why we are everlasting beings. That is why Nell the dog who was killed on a Somerset road still lives and waits. She is happy with loving people caring for her, until . . . But the great day will come when her master and mistress are with her—a family complete. Until then, she is loved and giving love and happy, perhaps hardly realising that one day she will be happier.

I remember a walk with Brother Peter in the 'Out of the Body' state when we met a group of little children singing and playing as they romped along the road. An Alsatian was with them, big, powerful, yet with those children he was as gentle as a lamb. When it was on the earth a boy was teasing it and it snapped at him, tearing his jacket, no doubt meaning to teach him a lesson. But the law decided that the dog was a menace and must be shot. It was surely the boy who should have been punished—the woman to whom it belonged wept and pleaded, but to no avail. If she could but see it now, she would stop grieving. Of course, she misses it. Of course, she realises that injustice was dealt out instead of justice, but it is so happy with children and they with it, where injustice and ignorance cannot reign. One day she will be with it again. When I think of that journey I can almost hear the dog's joyous barking, so impressed was it upon my memory.

I had a letter from a clergyman's widow yesterday and in it she tells me that recently she was sitting resting quietly in her favourite armchair, her eyes closed, but not asleep, when suddenly she felt her (departed) Airdale's head on her lap in its characteristic manner and, before she realised that it was a spirit manifestation, she was stroking it as naturally as if it had been there in the flesh. On a previous occasion, her husband (in the Spirit World) had been seen walking in the grounds of the vicarage with a favourite Irish terrier.

To give you some idea of the reality of astral travelling, may I tell you of an experience which is not connected with animals? I was travelling astrally and was seen clearly walking in Hampstead by four people who knew me personally, while my body was entranced in Canterbury. At this period I lived in West Hampstead. My landlady was a Mrs Martin. Her daughter was a member of my development circle. The Martin's lived on the ground floor of their house. My flat was at the top of the building. Miss Martin had a friend who lived in Richmond, a Mrs West. She was frequently a guest at the Martin's and whenever she was staying there she would say to Miss Martin, "Do ask Harold Sharp down and let him tell us of some of his psychic experiences." On the evening in question, Miss Martin replied, "Well, I am afraid he will not be able to come this time as he has gone to Canterbury for the weekend and will not be back until Tuesday."

On the Monday morning, I was booked to take charge of an investigation circle at the Canterbury Church, and Brother Peter entranced me and held me under control for over an hour talking, through me, to bring comfort to twelve bereaved sitters. It was at this time that, in West Hampstead, while Miss Martin was cooking the breakfast in the kitchen, Mrs West called out, "Mabel, I thought you said Harold Sharp was away for the weekend, he is not, he is just going down the steps from his own flat with his hat and cloak on." Hardly believing her ears, Miss Martin, frying pan in hand, came to the front window and saw me too. Just around the corner was a small home-made cake shop from which I regularly bought cakes. Mrs Margaret Harrison, the proprietor, was a member of my circle too—the same circle in which Miss Martin sat. Her assistant in the shop was a Mrs Jelly. Mrs Jelly was just arranging the cakes in the shop window when she saw me passing on the opposite side of the road and waved to me. "Who are you waving to?" enquired Mrs Harrison.

"Why, it's Harold Sharp going by as large as life with his cloak flying in the wind."

"It cannot be," said Mrs Harrison "He is taking the weekend services at Canterbury," and with her hands all covered with flour she came to the shop window and saw me. "He cannot have gone after all," she said, thinking this the only explanation. This was what we mean by astral travelling. Four people who knew me well saw me in Belsize Road at the same time precisely as twelve people in Canterbury were gathered together with me to hear one of those "Ministering Spirits sent to minister unto us," speaking words of comfort and wisdom through my lips, while I was entranced.

I can only guess why my spirit glided back to my flat while my body was safe in Brother Peter's keeping. The day before I left for Canterbury, I had had a telegram from the Edinburgh Psychic College asking if I could go there at very short notice as, owing to illness, the booked speaker had had to cancel his appointment. I wired to say I was engaged until Tuesday and offered to go on Tuesday evening if they wanted me. When I left for Canterbury, no answer had arrived and I can only guess that my real self was anxious to know what arrangements I had to make. I have no recollection of being in Belsize Road, but the four people who saw me were all thoroughly reliable people. They saw me individually at first, and a second person, in each case out of curiosity while still incredulous, came to their window and each of the four knew me and for years had seen and talked with me regularly.

That is much the sort of thing you do from time to time, though more than likely you travel to be with your loved ones in their spiritual home—telling them of your problems and asking their advice, rejoicing in their companionship, for there is no death and Heaven is very near. Your pets will no doubt find you out and race towards you with great excitement. Animals are often more psychic than humans. They seem to have fewer psychic inhibitions. No one has told them that it is wicked and not intended—so they use their faculty naturally. Have you never seen your dog or your cat suddenly gaze at some invisible creature and apparently watch their every movement with their eyes following them around the room?

I remember many years ago seeing a film which depicted with great truth this psychic ability of animals. A man in the Spirit World, seeing the unhappiness certain clauses in his Will was causing, visited his home to try to put matters right. The family concerned could not see him but his old faithful dog saw him and barked gladly and ran up to him just as though his master was still in the flesh. The humans not being psychic could not understand why the dog was so excited. Ah, I thought to myself, what a very true interpretation of an everyday occurrence, for the ever-living are frequently around us to bless and to cheer, not only the two-legged, but also the four-legged, and they that cleave the air with their wings do so also. If these fractions of Life are designed by the same Loving Father who designed us, should we not live in love and kindliness with them? Is not cruelty to them as inexcusable as cruelty towards one of our own kind?

I look and pray for the day when pity, compassion and mercy are the guiding virtues of mankind, when hunting and trapping and shooting and poisoning are but tales handed down from a barbaric age. An age when men at war bombed babes in cradles and hung their flags of victory in the Temples of the King of Love.

## OVERHEARD IN AN ORCHARD

Said the Sparrow to the Robin,
"I would really like to know
Why these restless human beings
Rush about and worry so?"

Said the Robin to the Sparrow
"Friend, I think that it must be
That they have no Heavenly Father
Such as cares for you and me."

Lightning Source UK Ltd.
Milton Keynes UK
UKHW01f1204220618
324641UK00011B/967/P